MODESTY

Clifton Fahie Jr

Fulton Books, Inc.
Meadville, PA

Published by Fulton Books 2021

ISBN 978-1-63710-861-1 (paperback)
ISBN 978-1-63710-862-8 (digital)

Printed in the United States of America

It was raining the way it rained around Lecanto, Florida. The job would have to be done no matter what. The dark purple Ferrari's light purple interior made the car a slight mauve. A car sometimes tells you about its driver's character, or it can be used to pull one away from the driver's character. The road of soldiers is often viewed as wider than it actually is. CIA officers never give in to the enemy.

Clifton Chow is known throughout the world for his charity donations that are usually hefty; his brand CU Chow is one of the world's leading designer brands. Having an honorary discharge from the navy, he then furthered his career in politics. Chow was pardoned after being convicted of contract killing (murder for hire) by the governor of Nevada after only two years into his sentence. Terrorists had tried to kill after abducting the son of a vodka tycoon. Proving that an honest man would break the law to protect his family, Mr. Chow, after returning the kid to his family, drove a red Bentley, wore red short pants, silk suit, kidnapped a Nazi, and a Kian member got them out of the car in front of the mirage in the street while traffic backed up and executed them both; he watched both of their corpses from beneath his Armani lens and waited as the cops came. After his release, he wrote a book, did some signing, ran for senate in Nevada, and won, so now he is officially known as Senator Chow.

Senator Chow has his eyes set on one of America's biggest prizes and that is the White House. Senator Chow and his beautiful wife met during their middle school years; actually, that is the time they became an item. Senator Chow and Divaress Chow would have just announced Senator Chow's run for president. Mr. Senator Chow would now start wearing black and gold tuxedos to represent Nevada. As a senator, he managed to have the Native Americans of Nevada's Reservation to be as pure as possible meaning with less outsider influence than ever—making him a legend politician that keeps his word and a champion among the people.

Juan Gulalado was once a seasoned star among his peers in Puerto Rican drug cartel. His snitching on transactions was about to meet punishment. It's been going on two years since Juan became a state witness. The trial of a Mexican cartel leader of Sinoala was scheduled to be held in thirty days in the federal court in New Jersey. Juan Gulalado used to wearing expensive linen, and his trademark were leather jackets. On this night, the night that his life would be the only fitpaument for his transgressions, Juan Gulalado was humiliated by his current attire. The results of being in witness protection. A red corduroy pants, sweater, and designer loafers a look he would have never been caught, *boom, boom, boom, boom*. Juan Gulalado's private parts had been shot off as he laid there with two holes in his chest and one in his head. "People like you are a disgrace to this country; you make money, get rich, get caught, and then want to get a pass by telling," said Senator Chow as he stood over Juan Gulalado's corpse.

Julius Anselmo was a computer wizard. Julius had already tapped into the city public camera system and took it down; he'd also took down the emergency response teams communications. "Senator Chow, you've got five minutes to get from there," said Julius.

"Sure thing, good friend," said Senator Chow, wearing tuxedo, a big Cuban link gold chain with a gold great white pendant for the wrist known as a Chappareta; he climbed in his purple Ferrari and was off on his way. Senator Chow was a man of integrity.

Julius Anselmo sent a text from what would read from unknown, but the text had read, "Like tamarind and tamales." And just like that, the Puerto Rican cartels' future was once again certain. The Puerto Rican cartel ruled with classic methods. Methods that made the federal government not eager to investigate the cartel. "Just a little more lipstick," Mrs. Chow said as she applied the last of her makeup. Mrs.

Chow was not at all away; she was always elegantly dressed. Divaress Chow is firm, kind, loving, and cold when time calls to be like that. "I hope this be the part where his ass gets shot," said Divaress Chow, speaking about her favorite daytime TV soap opera "Ghettoed."

"Yes," said Valkar Smith.

After the phone unsuccessfully didn't complete its first full ring. For Divaress Chow was making sure first and foremost that the senator was safe, the hackings were a success and with all of that had been done that the call had been more so the text had been made that the chicken was trimmed.

"Divaress, this successful contact is the forecast of our future; this was so freaking easy," said Valkar Smith.

"Sure thing," said Julius Anselmo.

"Valkar, had you heard from the senator?" asked Divaress Chow, already knowing the answer.

Valkar Smith was so grateful to know a Puerto Rican food producer spokesperson had just called and verified that yes they would be more than willing to be there, his campaign sponsors, so he was cheerful with slight question in his voice when he said no. Valkar Smith had long enjoyed wearing sweat suits. Tonight, he wore a Jordan and Nike Air sweat suit—one that's mostly black with stripe of lime green, pink, purple, and white with each brand's respected emblem and or its logo. Valkar Smith knew fighting against the NRA, going against global warming, having more counseling centers for youth instead of prison and proposing more so suggesting that prisons be used only to house sex offenders and deeply troubled mental health patients would ensure growth for the nation's economy. Senator Chow and Valkar Smith were magnificent calculative thinkers.

"I'll have the special," said the senator.

The waiter asked with a strong Brazilian accent asking, "Would that be all, senator?"

"Along with the special, give me a small portion of anything you feel is worth the while, and I'll cover the full cost and see that you are rewarded handsomely," said Senator Clifton Chow. "Excuse me waiter!" said the senator. "Divaress, you're so beautiful. I am the luckiest man in the world, and there is no one I'd rather share this journey that we would part take on."

"I love you," said Divaress.

She said it seductively while licking her teeth and did mean for it to be seductive. Divaress said what she to the senator after giving her order. It was so dainty; the waiter left immediately while Divaress spoke. During dinner, the Chows turned up. Divaress wore a Dolce & Gabanna evening wear. Divaress's earrings were done by Unusual James, and her shoes were Vera Wang. During such a night that's so successful, the senator's advisor clicked his computer and his pictures and information for his male expertise escort service blog. So he had already have ate, got his female guest that pertained to the genitals of males. Three females that came from the east that were very intriguing had arrived at the MGM. The advisor would be determined to make sure they all had met their peak climax.

The senator placed the extra virgin olive oil and placed it in front of his wife. He then stood made sure he hadn't been creased then walked until he stood behind his wife. Senator Clifton Chow raised her hair bent and licked and smacked his lips on her neck then reached for the olive oil. Senator Clifton Chow started to rub the oil in his hands, putting his right hand on top of his wife's had and his left hand obtained the container of oil that he placed on the table.

"Ahh," Divaress sighed, rolling her head. Rubbing from atop her head two and a half minutes after the senator was at her temples for two and a half minutes after being there, he then moved to her neck; her nipples were advantageous to her beautiful Dolce & Gahanna wear.

"Diva will be treated like a diva," said Senator Chow.

Divaress by this time would have turned a key and press the buttons for nuclear action to have Senator Clifton Chow stick some dick in her right this minute. Julius Anselmo was still motivated and with good reason; the three females were gorgeous. Julius smoked on a cigar as he rolled a joint that persist of some bright yellow cannabis. He poured some vodka on the cigar sheet and rocked a little way as Diana Ross song played low at an elegant tone. The three danced by ways if shaking their waist slowly in lingerie that was extremely feminine. For a man that is a heterosexual, that is the grail of dreams. Locked in by Julius licking his blunt, the lady in the middle went on her knees then crawled on her knees to the man with the plan. The other two ladies sprayed whip cream on her while she continued to crawl. The lingerie would look like it would anytime now lodge in her crevis and bite on her coochie. Julius knew after this job's posting on his blog, he would have clients. So much clients so that this quarter would prove to be his dominant by far. Julius Anselmo, advisor to Senator Clifton Chow, does his best to avoid clients that seek extreme bondage and licks. Whether receiving or sharing, that was a big no-no. Julius would not let anything risk his political agenda. Because in politics, he knew all scandals were treated as big ones.

Divaress orgasms were all heavy, and she had left puddles everywhere they had smashed. The hotel's staff would always donate the face towels in a quantity that would be enough for the diner. The diner didn't lose either because the Chows always used the towels to wipe the puddles dry and left five stacks for staff every place they had left a puddle. The staff always sanitized the diner after the power couple left the premise. Senator Chow and Divaress enjoyed their love life. Vroom, vroom! The purple Ferrari was ready to hit the Vegas Blvd and its occupants. The rims were all shining. Clifton Chow and Divaress Chow ride home was magnificent like always they mattered to each other and so did each other's opinion. So occasionally they held hands with each other while the senator drove.

"So next week, we go and start to introduce the world; to introduce the next president of the United States of America was a big statement," said Divaress.

"The first state we'll stop at is Florida; that one case about the two Republicans and one Independent congress members is a good start," said Senator Chow.

"Swamp are a natural occurrence, so our slogan pertaining to that matter would have a Caribbean twist to it," said Divaress.

"What would that be?" asked Clifton Chow.

"Please help us keep our swamps lean," replied Divaress.

"With the donations for the campaign already being made, that automatically leaves no room for financial sanity deprivation," said Senator Clifton Chow.

"Anyone of those cops accused of killing an unarmed black person. If they have any form of hate on their property, I am cooking the shit and taking it to their asses," said Divaress.

"God never put humans in the world to hate over color," said Senator Chow.

"If we do get any dogs, if and when your elected were getting pit bulls," said Divaress.

"The leopards take their kill up in a tree to ration their rations so we must preserve the innocent of this great country," said Divaress.

"A man is not a sinner in the eyes of God if he didn't know while committing an act of wrong doing, it was wrong," said Divaress.

Just then, the senator was just on their properties driveway. They will take a shower in their own showers for tonight. Being that they both wanted to be both rested because the day ahead they'd be facing they wanted to be rested. They would feed each other dried tropical fruits hat were dry. Then they would go to sleep. The day has a lot in store for the power couple. They were both in tune with the meek part of each of their spirits. Senator Clifton Chow was used to being defender of himself. Even though none of security nor his bodyguards could whip his ass, it was somewhat relieving. Just the fact of him being a politician elected the American government would make his safety a priority.

The head of Chow's security team was Chico Vern; he was a scrapper from young. Chico grew up with the Chows. That was important because they chose to surround themselves with people that knew how cops worked. Chico left Vegas at age twelve because he fought often. He was sent to Chicago where he mastered Tai Chi and curbed his temper. Chico was welcomed back to Vegas with opened arms by his mother whom sent him away out of love. Chico graduated with good grades. So security is the way he chose to cash in on his fighting skills. Chico now really knew his importance to country of his birth by heading the security detail for a man that would be of significance. The Bentley Continental was being prepared for

Senator Chow. It was such a beautiful machine. The outside was rimmed with nine plated rims with cream body. The interior was dark silver. *Security detailing should not be hard because nobody ever wants to harm a senator*, Chico thought. While the cars were being prepared, Divaress and Clifton slept the night away.

"A night of sleep for the Chows are almost instant sunshine," said Clifton.

Clifton popped the mouthwash bottle, took a mouthwash, swished it around for some seconds, and spat it out inside a party cup that was on the bedside. Clifton reached for the ashtray and lighter. *Fuh.*

Clifton toked the joint was lit. The taste reminded him why he always let a joint rolled and halfway burned. "Wooh," said Clifton as he the senator exhaled some smoke. The senator took a toke on the joint while he stood in front of Divaress's bedroom door. Clifton stood admiring her then he left. He was about to start to get prepared for a moment that could be considered a miracle in ways that a lot of people would have to agree with. Politicians are elected by the people causing the people to expect the politicians to keep their word. When the people find a politician like the senator, the people tend to support them fully.

"Senator Chow, everything is in order; tracking, distress signal, and oil slick," said Chico. "Should we prepare another car for the pleasure of Mrs. Chow?" asked Chico.

"I honestly don't know, Chico; I think you should ask her," said Clifton.

Chico texted Divaress asking so he offered no suggestion on how she traveled before or how she should travel now. Divaress texted that she would enjoy the day better if she had traveled with her lover. So, like a brother, Chico took the text to Senator Clifton Chow. Knowing Clifton would find this enchanting, he showed the senator the text. And the senator beamed like he was still in grade school. Chico wore a tuxedo also; it was black on black while his employees wore all white.

"All right, let's do this straight to the airport," said the Senator Clifton Chow.

The lears that awaited the entourage had rose petals leading all the way to the doorway.

"I would be there in fifteen minutes and under," said Valkar Smith.

Valkar hung up the phone, disconnecting from the Senator Clifton Chow. Valkar Smith was reciting parts of his speech concerning global warming. He looked at himself in the mirror in his tuxedo and felt relaxed and amused by his grandup reflection. To look the part and be dedicated to the part is something that gives one character. Valkar had reached, and they all shook hands. Everyone was offered a shot of scotch by a lady that obtained a tray. Lots of scotch in shot glasses she walked to and fro while they all took and returned their shot glasses. Senator Clifton Chow held Divaress hand and began toward the steps.

"All aboard," said Senator Clifton Chow as he couldn't help but to smile.

"We should be in Florida in about six hours," said Chico.

One of Chico's employees could fly jets also. With such important cargo having a guard who also knows how to fly is good security protocol.

"Florida is a state that is already there for talking for any politician that has a proven track record, Julius Anselmo. And that's where we come in," said Divaress.

The pilot did his basic aviator's introduction and instructions with a few kinks and bends with the acceptation of the flight being a private flight. The flight attendant was in the middle of the aisle doing and saying the things flight attendants do along with looking beautiful. The flight was mostly conversation about preparations for speeches formation of deliberations, structure for entrance, note for the auditorium's pedestrians, drinks, food, shirts, slogans, interior designs, parking lot supervision, valet parking for the VIP, etc.; fried chicken, mashed potatoes that were homemade, biscuits, and carrot cake with ice cream was the meal served after the first hour of flight. During the meal, there hadn't been much conversation. Due to the fact that who wasn't asleep, wasn't doing anything mostly other than overlooking their notes. Divaress was making sure like divas and that had been to make sure her sexy was on. There was some rap music by a Compton artist that played. That song like the others that played was from both crews selected playlist.

"Three more hours of the Gulf huh, boss. Eating those fried chickens made those last couple of hours feel like forty-five minutes to me," said Chico.

"Yes, indeed," said Valkar Smith. "I would like some Chinese food on this go around. Have you ever had Russian food, Baltic food, and or Middle Eastern, Mr. Vern?" asked Valkar Smith.

"Sometimes, well actually most times good tasting food is not healthy," said head of security.

"Such a short while we have to live, live while you're alive because good food is always fulfilling to the soul, Mr. Chico Vern," said Valkar Smith.

Divaress reached up and pushed the button overhead summoning the stewardess. Divaress nails were red, and one of her nails was a chow chow designed out of diamonds.

"Would you like a fruit salad and a glass of Don P on the side, Mrs. Chow the beautiful?" asked Shirley the stewardess.

"You know what?" asked Divaress. "I had just called you for some liquor, but I'll just take you up on that fruit salad," said Divaress.

Divaress had just wiped the last of the mouthwash from on her lips and comers of her mouth. Divaress thought for a second and thought, *Damn there ain't no way around.*

Senator Clifton Chow had just finished up with his hygiene. Wiped his mouth and side of his lips with his hands and after that rubbed his hands together with hand sanitizer that he'd just applied. And just like that Divaress had thought her horny Jennie had not disappoint at a high altitude, and he'd just rose out of the bottle. So, in the lounge section, Divaress was being foreplayed for the big play. It went down like this. They were romantically taste buds breeding and with Senator Clifton Chow on top. They seemed to be making angels. *Flll.* Now the Victoria Secret was on the side. Rawdawg your wife for life is how the Chow's played ball. The senator jammed it up in his wife; in other words, he gave her all the sausage in the aisle. After ten hard strokes, he then stuck his tongue in her ear. Now lick-

11

ing her neck, the senator spun Divaress over on her stomach, gave her five strokes then lift her up while she moaned, he pounded her pussy like a phone ringing, matter of fact, like an oil rig. They both emerged from the lounge to applause.

The stewardess then announced there will be shrimp fried rice with fried plantains, cherry pie for dessert, and Maubi, an island beverage. "We got less than three hours, and we'll be flying over the state of our destination," said Shirley.

Shirley started sharing the food and then she proceeds to share the plates out. All the occupants waited until everyone received their food.

"Thank you, God, for this food," said Clifton Chow.

Everyone begun eating. Chico was not having any problems using his chopsticks. All the others used utensils. Chico made a note to himself to know who the caterer for the flight had been. *The broccoli and plantains had set a new level,* he thought while running through his meal.

"Everybody, eat all you can; it's going to be a hard day upon arrival. We all know each other, forget about acting cute. Also, when you doing it for real, don't forget me," Shirley said.

Everyone had laughed. For Shirley knew, she was family to the Chows and to the staff. They had flown over Tampa already, so by now, game faces were just about on. Upon arrival, they had already discussed that Divaress and Clifton Chow would drive separate cars.

Clifton chose a white Bugatti with chrome, creme, and white was tired. Divaress chose a pink Lamborghini with pink and white rims. Coffee and relaxation and they'll feel sober. Shirley gave everyone a Gatorade and a five-hour energy so that energy may somewhat be replenished. The security team would be in all black Cadillac SUVs, and Chico would be in a white one. Glock 40 with clip, vest, and 2 forty round drums were the apparel guarantee for each guard. Now Chico would use this time to go over pictures and blueprints of the facility. Detail by detail, Mr. Verne would go over it with his team. After that, Chico would go over the escape routes with Chow's staff. Chico felt confident everyone knew what to do in case of emergency. Chico had also felt confident with the feeling they all would give theirs, and also everybody knew their job and or jobs. Enough so to do it at their best. The landing gear could be heard and felt as it protruded through the bottom of the plane.

"Shirley, would you be so kind to keep your line open up for me please?" asked Divaress.

"Sugar, you know I am down," said Shirley.

"Look, you just observe everything you have to use it as a tool to know your surroundings and to keep your nerves calm," said Shirley.

"Peace be to you!" was said by the aviation team. The politicians and their staff had returned the aviation crews' farewell to them light heartedly. So now the staff was now in Miami.

"We'll make it with time to spare," Chico said.

He spoke to the entire staff about their diligence, and Chico stated it, matter of fact with what appeared to be no concern. "Mr. Senator Clifton Chow and Divaress, I know you guys, and I know you guys are capable of accomplishing what lies ahead."

Everyone then loaded up in their respected seating positions to the rides they had been assigned, whether they'd be solo or not. All the cars had now started to roll off one behind the other. It was a neat array of cars mostly armored in the motorcade. Miami was a city of a whole lot of different cultures. With beauty everywhere, sometimes even the hoods shared some of the limelight. Clifton Chow, at one time during the night, had the Bugatti up three digits on the speedometer at least once for the trip. The car helped him to relax. It was a beautiful and colorful scene of beautiful dresses of elegance cars and SUVs along with tuxedos. Valet helped the ladies to their feet upon exiting the vehicles and were handed the keys. The valets were handed the keys from the males while they held their doors as they exited. Everyone gave themselves the once over and seemed to be content with what they'd seen.

Senator Clifton Chow and Divaress Chow met by a double door which had had a lit sign above it that read "Entrance." They held each other's hand while security guards, one each, opened a door. Both of them greeted the Chows while they greeted them back. While the doors were being held, some of the armed guards walked in behind the couple. The mood wasn't grim; it was an atmosphere where things of great significance would be addressed and acknowl-edged. Were they all would someday like to look back and say we did it, we got the job done.

The hall hadn't been cramped; they have rugged walls and floors. Air-conditioning was set more on the cold side. The rugging was a velvet blue soothing jazz came from speakers beneath the rugging.

"Good evening, ladies and gentlemen; my name is Julius Anselmo, and for those of you who don't know who I am, I'm the advisor of Senator Clifton Chow," said Julius Anselmo.

"Senator Clifton Chow as short as his role as a senator has brought new ideas to our state. He even got bills that are authentic that had failed in the past to be passed that benefited the state," said Julius.

"One of my personal favorites the senator had brought was to create new gutter at the north east and south of Nevada and had them directed to nearby deserts and canyons of neighboring state; now our state has seen a large drop in flood related devastation," said advisor Julius Anselmo.

Julius had had to wait for around ten seconds for the applause was of a large and lengthy scale. Julius Anselmo then continued with some holograms of Senator Chow doing things within the commu-nity such as helping an elderly woman cross the street by getting out of his hot pink 2004 Range Rover with his jewelry on. One that was another crowd favorite was of the senator rescuing a little girl's kitten from up a tree while he wore a white based Louis Vuitton shorts and matching top and tennis shoes. The senator was holding the kitten while the little girl smiled while she rubbed the top of the kitten's head, and during all of this, the senator had kissed his forest green Julius Caesar; that its interior was light yellow with chrome interior accessories, red floor with red mats. The light-yellow interior was flawless accompanied by the red shock and red brake pads.

Valkar Smith sat between two aspiring actresses that wore dresses by Sergio Valente with accessories by Uncommon James.

"Good evening, America; this is World News," said the broad-caster while "Breaking News" ran at the bottom of the screen and "Live" was at the top of the screen in the corner. "We have word from our source that tells us a Las Vegas senator is in Miami with supporters waiting for him to make a major announcement any time soon. Our sources say the senator's staff is tight lipped," said the reporter.

There were major news networks locked outside also accompanied by local stations looking for a story. Chico Vern stood in front of the news teams and asked them the obvious, which was would they like to partake with what was getting ready to occur. Before the bidding frenzy started, Chico the calculated genius signaled the security doorman to weapons search all the media personnel that had entered the marble and mirrored lobby styled hallway—a storm of media to which most headed for the front of the stage. Julius Anselmo knew for someone so beloved there was only one way only to do this.

Sources are telling us the senator may have a grave illness and might want to get treatment in the state of Florida seeking an early retirement, enjoying the last of a great life on the Atlantic and Gulf Coast while being an occasional advisor to the president was some stations one of many assumptions. Valkar Smith and Relaxptia Smith held hands, a lovely couple. Senator Clifton Chow and Divaress came out right after the Smiths. There were three podiums with a mic and a chair. One of the podiums and its mic was being used by Julius as he'd introduced the couple both by names of first and spousal last.

"People, I give you Senator Chow," said Julius Anselmo.

Julius had assured everyone the senator, his family, and staff was all in good health. The advisor also told the people and media that the senator has plans drawn and ready to take the state of Georgia for a thoroughbred racetrack. Something so lucrative would be expected to be picked up by the Breeders' Cup. A business he had told them would generate thousands of new jobs and hundreds of billions of dollars if not more would boost the academy and political leaders must agree it would only keep the economy healthy.

"Yes, thank you very much; you'll be giving a lot more applauses before the night is done," assured Clifton Chow. "I've invited my followers and media because it's a good year so let's see if we could make it better. With no further delay, I am running for president," said Chow. Applause erupted and it felt as though even the planet had rejoiced. The great leader the people had long deserved. Intelligent a true tree hugger and a carnivore if need be. Senator Chow held Divaress's hand, she stood, he then sat as she approached the podium.

Divaress spoke through the mic on things such as when she first met her husband. Divaress's nails sparkled. It was easy to see why Senator Chow had married her. Divaress was striking and elegant; she was like watching a raindrop drop on a needle or watching a drop fall on an eye of a sewing needle.

"The Senator Clifton Chow and I had times that tried us on our way to you the people of this nation; the journey to this podium was with to fulfill the works to benefit nature and people," said Divaress.

Divaress had said the country was yes doing all right it was now time at hand for it to do great. "It's time as a nation we trod taking over the world and not stomping on anybody's toes," she said.

Divaress felt strict gun laws weren't more important than keeping schools safe. Divaress felt more mics and cameras on school campuses would help to make accusations of bulling be more substance, causing most mass shooters had felt they'd been the black sheep.

Reality is everyone already had negative thoughts before d e to being bullied, some act out their thoughts. Situations being monitored usually end with more likable and reasonable solutions.

Divaress felt terrorists were cowards due to the fact that the military trained to beat was with terrorists. But nine times out of ten, the terrorists never make a blunt attack on the military.

"To terrorist, if you want to war with our military, we will welcome the wars be real warriors and leave the community out the war," said Divaress.

The audience, some shook their heads in agreement while they applauded, someone even shouted "Amen," and the others just applauded. Some young people could be wise beyond their years. Divaress is proof that such theories are conclusions. The crowd applauded while Divaress thanked them and went to be sated. With about two more steps toward the chair, the senator rose, offered his hand to Divaress. Divaress sat while the senator stood on her left side.

"Valkar Smith is my name, and part of my expectance is to serve as your vice president and be part of an administration that earn your trust," said Valkar Smith. He pulled on his tuxedo. "So then I could then go ahead after that and be as good as a president that I know Senator Chow will be," said Valkar Smith.

The audience clapped at Valkar's speech.

"Our nation is being built every day with the expectations that drams would be reached. This nation is known as the land of the free, so we have to find a resolution to our country despite that being the world's leader in inmate incarceration. Too much of taxpayers' money is being spent that could be used to build a better nation," said Valkar Smith.

Cheers had now been abundant. Valkar usually spoke his inner feelings. Valkar spoke also about education saying yes kids should be definitely computer literate but pencils, pens, and paper must always be part of our countries educational system's structure. Applause were being heard. Valkar Smith walked away from the podium after thanking the audience all forms of audience. He then stood in front of Relaxptia offering her his hand; she accepted, she stood, and he walked her to the podium.

Then Valkar adjusted the mic for his (Relaxptia) as he sometimes called her. Valkar's destination right after that was the same exact chair Mrs. Smith had sat in.

"Greetings to all; my name is Relaxptia Smith, and I am willing to stand by my husband as he says this country next to Mr. chow if they are given the chance by U and I would be a strong first lady if ever given a chance by such a great nation. As a nation, we are not going to fail our children; we would protect our children their future and the environment. I grew up with my great-grandmother telling me how you could leave doors unlocked when she was growing up, and everything would be where you'd left it. Shit, I would love to tell stories like those. Only stories from back in the days I heard I would want to be telling are the ones you old school know," said Relaxptia.

Some people had got up cheering for Mrs. Smith as she clicked a pen on her bottom left sharp teeth as she stroked her weave doing a half sashay. One news anchor had said to his audience when it had beeped that this is how live television can be at times; he had said it light heartedly.

"You know everybody that watched and heard what you was saying, 'Know you got real ass chick all over your ass, Divaress,'" through the staff's earpiece Shirley had said. "Told you, I got your back," Shirley said.

"I know you the truth girl don't even trip," said Divaress.

"If and when we get to look out for our country, I will start a family then knowing to myself a positive foundation was set, and I'd been a part of its process," said Shirley.

Chico Vern had asked if he could be the godparent of Shirley's kid or kids. Shirley ran her hand through her weave while laughing telling Chico ain't nobody was talking to his ass. Chico was looking all smooth like a sheet of new loose-leaf paper with a cooler response, which was him saying he knows Shirley would make a good mother.

"Aw, that's so sweet of you," said Shirley.

Shirley had at the same wiped a tear from her right eye with her pinkie finger mostly with a backhand fashion.

"Chico, you even security with the tongue. I can see," said Divaress. She covered her mouth. The three of them enjoyed a quick laugh.

"We will strive to keep schools and the recreation park with equipment and extras round the clock. Something we also plan to see corrected is every full-time teacher has a start salary of fifty thousand dollars a year. We must treat our children with great importance by making sure they are comfortable and also their teachers. We have even tried and also submitted data on coral growth and growths maintenance," said Relaxptia. Mrs. Smith had tried some experiments with and environmental corporation named Green Block. "Reached good conclusions pertaining to environmental rehabilitations what we did at Green Block. If the government ok's it now, we can start helping the environment as of now," said Relaxptia.

The local news and major news outlets were trying to get each detail of what each speaker was saying. These people that spoke had been perceived to have confidence in all and everything they said. If what they're claiming is true on broadcast had said that from Sin City comes Guardian Angels. The senator, Julius, Divaress, Valkar, Relaxptia, and a spokeswoman for Green Block gave closing statements. The campaign after party destination had been mentioned and had been muted by all-news station. Opening campaign trail had kicked off with what had felt like success. Countries around the world had shown photos of Senator Chow, his wife, and his immediate political circle. They were all eager because of the things they related very much too much of his wants—one hand washing the other.

The caterers for the event were requested to be in ordinance to have ten plates with everything, ten plates with desserts, and ten bottles of Rozay, ready to go. Those orders would be transported to the aviation staff at the airport.

"How are you doing baby?" asked Amateia. "I ain't even get to see you when I was watching the news, and I looked everywhere. Everyone that spoke on the podium speech was very encouraging and moving. I love you so much that you probably be smiling to yourself sometimes saying my *amor es lavida loca*," Amateia said.

"You know I love all the attention you be giving me, and it ain't no other woman for me, I could tell you that," Chico elocuted to Mrs. Vern.

Tonight, Senator Clifton Chow would mingle and converse with guests for nearly fifty minutes. Ten minutes, he will use to give a speech congratulating everyone for their efforts and sacrifices. Then he will summon a few—to be precise a select group of people because there was work to be done. The more progress, the more results. A software engine and electronics designer had met and conversated with Relaxptia, Valkar, and Senator Clifton Cow. With corporations having new designs every year, they felt the time was right to discuss recycling old gadgets and disposing them globally. How this should be done they thought putting the world in four sections, and every section during a seasonal quarter, its residents would bring their waste and have it weighed and be paid.

"Of course, we'll be shelling out at least one billion dollars a year a small price for such a meaningful cause. If we get all major tee corporations to donate that is a-five-hundred-million-dollar start not to mention every company would be giving an equal percentage is not an option of the material after it was recycled and ready to be remolded," said Relaxptia.

Meanwhile, Divaress was speaking to a construction and heavy trucking operator and owner. They had been juggling ideas back and forth he was mid-50s, 5'8, well groomed, his hair braided, and both of his parents he said came from Nigeria. They both felt that baron projects depending on their locations could be transferred to different things. Some places could be used to plant eatable foods for residents of such city or cities that have its less fortunate people. A park could be for some others. Some got the potential to have petting zoos. Others could be redesigned. Reconstruction would also mean the conservation of wildlife. And other suggestions await.

"Good evening, ladies and gentlemen; tonight has proven to be an epic one, but we have things we need to get done," said Julius Anselmo.

They all sat around a round white marble table. Only those from the staff's core were allowed behind the doors to this conference which were more of an organized meeting.

"Brugus Towski is a former Russian mafia that's now trying, well actually has a lucrative hustle going on, and it consists of him dumping waste in the Everglades of Florida. We have destiny on our side; for one is the mafia doesn't believe in pollution, and the main thing is he's no longer part of the Russian mafia. He set up a meeting with our representative because he thinks he'll be able to back us in a corner and make us cower. He is known to have two bodyguards of his in tow at all times; they both are over two hundred pounds," said Julius. The two men's fate will be made accordingly. "These guys are kind of nice; their fault was being in acquaintance with Brugus Towski, so they get to have a funeral. Do you know sources reported to us that the last oil spill in the Gulf was organized by Brugus Towski?" asked Julius Anselmo. "Since he likes to destroy nature, we will set aside a special punishment for this one," Julius Anselmo said.

By the way, this meeting/conference was going Miami's murder rate was going up tonight for sure. Miami's night life would serve as an accomplice.

"Any other bodyguard of Towski's would be taken out if he had any others if they are in the clear and if they pose a threat to what we have to accomplish. Tonight is a night his ass won't have any delays on meeting the heal of Allah," said Julius. Mr. Anselmo when he had just said he had been referring to Brugus Towski. "Chico, I want the best that you've got out there with you not anyone who's need more than two shots max," said Julius.

Chico Vern nodded his head in acknowledgment—a posse of old cars with big rims, loud car sets, and each with a different color.

"However, the job is done let his head be the last to go," said Relaxptia.

At the Hilton, Senator Clifton Chow and Divaress Chow waited in the theater that was turned to resemble a conference room. Down or more so in the lobby, head of security staff waited with two of his top men. Chico Vern knew in order to maneuver and kill the snake the snakes head must always be seduced by the predator. A strong Russian accent complaining of how much money he'd spent in the hotel, and in his opinion, how he should be immediately recognized and be treated.

"Look, you people may feel you Americans may think the world is yours, but you must know you'll never have Russia," said Brugus Towski.

"There are thirteen of these shit marbles in all. Brugus came with the two he was expected to be with and ten of his men are in front the hotel and its perimeters with two of them in front of a vehicle," said Chico.

"All right, Chico; let's put feet in Brugus ass like peas," said Shirley.

"Men to your assigned station; ready your weapon and remember one shot," said Chico.

"We are prepared to kill, and we have been trained and groomed by the best the business has to offer," said a lower ranking security personnel.

The moment Chico gave the word; silencers had started to be worked by large rifles.

Brugus Towski's men, a total of eight were lying in a pool of blood, their own blood. The two of Brugus Towski's hitters that were in front of the car was heading for cover and in the motion of drawing more so reaching for their guns. Chico's men swatted their asses down like waves kicking sand on a shoreline's ass. Any coming traffic toward the hotel would be intercepted by men who will not let unknown people discover the bodies before the appropriate time.

Brugus Towski's goons opened the doors for their boss and trailed behind him. Ten feet inside the conference room and with each of the goons side by side of each other and at a length of three feet behind their boss. A total of four men approached the Russian and his hitters to whom looked like they knew it would be a no-hit game for their team. Two of Chico's men held guns on the trio while a next man relieved them of their weapons. Chico also had his gun and silencer pointed at the trio.

"Don't you, two boys, worry your families would be seeing you soon," said Chico.

"Take them through the back door," said Senator Clifton Chow.

Knowing if he's spoke some of the topics to Towski that frustrated him in the goon presence, they'll still think it's a meeting.

"So you want not only to complain but to humiliate me as well. I would not forget of this, senator," said Brugus. Apparently, Towski thought the situation he is in, and the one he was facing would be intense arguing at the max at Towski's words Relaxptia laughed.

The two goons when led to the porch didn't notice their situation quick enough. Thin cheap rugs were on top of the plastic, so Towski didn't see nothing to note as suspicious when the door opened the two men hadn't broke stride. Two of the security on the porch of the adjoining room held the door; the one of the other two closed the door, and the other ordered the goons to wait. After the door was closed, the hitters were then ordered to proceed. They both, meaning the goons, walked in unison. *Bloom, sploo, sploo.* Back at the side part of their head, the men were shot. The carpet and the bodies were organized within the plastic quick enough and reliable enough to avoid plasma leakage.

"Chico and them is going to kick Towski's ass to the point where his teeth are going to be kissing his ass to the point where they'll be begging his ass to let them reach back to his mouth," said Shirley.

Divaress walked up to Towski and back hand him. Relaxptia then back handed the shit out of his ass.

"In my country, you, ladies, would've been my farm girls," said Brugus Towski.

Senator Clifton Chow stood with his hands in his pockets without saying a word. In the meantime, Brugus was shot by Chico from a tranquilizer. The security team rushed to him before he could make a loud make a loud thud while he fell. The two goons' corpses were snuck down to the parking lot where the carpet and plastics would then be disposed of, but their bodies would lay with others to be discovered by or identified by authorities.

The two men placed the canoes in the water; it was a spooky place with long grass. Wer and the edge of the most deadly natural environment in the world, the Everglades. Brugus's tranquilized frame was loaded between the two men on the canoe where he lay. With two canoe rowing college champions rowing for fifteen consecutive minutes, they were good ways in the Everglades.

Other members of the senator's team had been there feeding some gators. The men were giving some of the gator's names. One of the men shined the light back further from a group of gators they had been feeding. And then the holder of the flashlight swore and pointed and told his comrades to look. They all gasped at the sight nature had just gave them. It was a fourteen-feet gator on the clutches of a really large Burmese python. The canoe reached the bank. The cargo was unloaded. Brugus would be put to sit upright where his hands would be tied at his sides. The river boat one of them had been prepared. The men use alcohol and smacked Brugus around a couple of times until he had come around. Towski asked where he was at. He was answered. A little bit of fear sat in, but Brugus shoot it off.

"Mr. Towski, you strike me as a man that doesn't have love any species or for our environment," said Chico.

Brugus proceed to elocute of a time he was in India was attacked in its jungle by a fifteen-feet king cobra and killed it with a Zulu Nation's spear.

"I tell you what, Brugus, I am willing to risk everything. We will let you hang waist deep in the water with this lasso; I just fastened around your shoulders. If in five minutes nothing tries to eat you, you'll be hauled up and back in Miami," said Chico.

"Bait I am now. I would like to know if your word would be kept? I am a very powerful man with powerful friends, Chico," Towski said.

"I know, Mr. Towski. The lights," said Chico.

"Death was basically already visible, Mr. Towski. I think that snake would have that gator tonight; look at that gator as one less mouth that could bite your ass, Brugus. Load it up boys!"

The men then begun to bring Brugus to his feet and had him carried onto the river boat. The python was almost completely through strangling the alligator that was about fifteen feet from where the riverboat was, its crew and its occupant. Brugus was in the water where his elbows had been slightly submerged for roughly going on a minute and a half. None of the gators had nudged him much less bit him. Brugus, during this time, was trying to have Chico and his men engage in small talk. Brugus would speak insults as if he somehow thought the men salivated from and by his insults. He's started to elocute on how he'll hunt them down then the monster from below pulled on him; the men pulled him to where his head was above water. Brugus had gasped to catch his breath which was futile because he was grabbed again. The gators began feeding while Brugus was screaming, and the men shot him with adrenaline. Brugus was alive enough to feel himself be eaten. When Brugus was screaming because his toes to his pelvis. Chico was all smiles looking at Brugus. An eighteen-feet gator came up while Brugus was screaming and had the last.

Valkar Smith was aware of the fact his wife was a nature lover, but he didn't know she could be a savage to protect nature.

Chico, Vern, and his team were heading back at the hotel area. So the media and the cops would be there because those bodies left to be found would be or should be found anytime now. Brugus Towski was gone. Relaxptia, Julius, Divaress, Chico, and Senator Chow had all congratulated each other. Chico and his team had already had a bottle back inside the hotel and its property. Knowing that the media and news reporters would want to ask him and some staff members questions.

Senator Chow stayed with the others who had been there with those who was in the spot with him waiting on Chico them to return. One of Chico's men had said through his earpiece, "Valkar Smith was being questioned by the cops." Chico had them reached through the air system undetected. Knowing what lay ahead the men regrouped themselves and formed their regular security formation around the senator and his staff and headed out. Upon arrival in the lobby, cameras flashed through the glass on the staff. Different Ds called different staff members asking some of the same and various questions. After they all aced the questions, they exited the lobby. The media was promised a half hour worth of cooperation from any and all staff members.

Valkar Smith was already outside answering the media's questions; when he saw his wife, he ran toward her and embraced her.

Senator Chow then begun by sending his condolences to the love ones of the deceased. Various but the most frequent was did Senator Chow see this as an attempt on his life and his staff. The senator wrapped up all after by saying him and his staff wouldn't ease up even if it was then saying he didn't plan to keep Massachusetts people longer than two days. "Once again, my condolences to anyone who'd lost someone here tonight," said Senator Clifton Chow. Senator Chow wished everyone a good night. Chico and his men lead the convoy on the way to the airport in Miami.

Shirley and Amateia mostly spoke through the earpieces. Shirley gave them the menu for breakfast which was pumpkin fritters and king fish with lemon grass tea. Amateia told them the forecast prediction of their flight. Valkar Smith was contemplating and dictating meeting for the next two months.

Each of the staff members boarded the aircrafts. Chico and four of his men would emerge from the jet in Ocala, Florida. The instructions would already be given. There was an officer who had shot two unarmed black youths and had also killed an Asian, Spanish, and White kid from a trailer park. All the equipment would be waiting in the given area. Chico had boarded the plane before the four security goons left. After the work gets smashed by them, they'll return to this same spot on Orlando's airport where a private owned 757 would be awaiting them to connect them with staff up on the northeast.

Jerry Boot was in a gray and white robe beneath was a gray pinstriped with pajamas. Jerry Boot had a white mug in his right hand; he was taking sips of his coffee from. Jerry Boot was going to the front of his lawn to retrieve the rubber banded and rolled newspaper. Two cars, luxury cars with two passengers in each on both side, Boot had one of these cars traveling toward Boot, twenty-five meters from Boot was the cars going twelve miles per hour. A driver and shooter were the occupants. The shooters each were armed with M-16s with silencers. From forty feet on Boot's left and right by his mailbox, he stooped to get his paper when the shots were penetrating his head and torso. Only five shots from each rifle were fired. The guns were stolen from his neighbor's house months ago. After Boot was shot, the guns were thrown on his lawn. The shooter that shot him from the backseat worked his way to the front seat for the passenger as he could. Two blocks away, they switched cars and the passengers before had now been driving to Orlando's airport.

So Massachusetts was a large state with a tough crowd, known for their don't-take-crap attitude. Senator Chow felt that if there were any people, he would appeal to Massachusetts is that place.

The Quadro was now on the stairs to go on the plane. Now, with Jerry a thing of the past, the men felt accomplished.

A neighbor of Jerry Boot seen him on the lawn on his stomach with both his legs up leaned against the mailbox surrounded in crimson. She screamed a scream that was terrifying but was extra frightening at such hours in the morning. Some kids watched through windows while others had to be ushered back indoors several times. One adult called the police, while some watched on as others conversated with others. The Ds reached the scene and moments after so did the coroners and the meat wagon. The Ds were padding crime scene details surveying Boot's house and asking residents and neighbors questions to which no one knew the answers. Hate had once again been ousted by a righteous cause.

Some days, Floridian skies could be miles and miles of no turbulence and high visibility.

Other day, it's like being in a flying blender. So, by time Divaress's them flight hits North Florida, the four gentlemen of their friends Chico's security squad that had stayed back to handle up on the Boot proposition would be around thirty minutes out Orlando flight time. The men had a hot breakfast and had had shots of cane rum and washed it all down with some Don Perigon.

Divaress had been discussing them any and all of those that may be a proposition that needed to be dealt with. There had been five names that had been in the red.

Valkar Smith had been making a flight plan of cities; he felt would be a place to now turn to on the way back to the state of Nevada. Valkar was drinking a round of black liquor. A trip to Denmark would be great when all of this is going through with was one of the thoughts that ran through Valkar's mind.

During the flight, cocktails shots, beers, and martinis were in full flight rotation like a pro football championship victory celebration. Snack were being consumes like that of a pot bowl. Divaress thought Georgia was a place good enough to introduce the world to peach gin. Divaress had thought the city of mobile could be a great place to reintroduce a part of Decatur's culture to Mobil. Senator Chow wanted a peaceful presidency one with no war, chaos, and or unnecessary strife. So, although they all shared drinking conversations, everyone was together but still alone in thought. Massachusetts cold, with a big city a few successful sports teams had notorious reputation for being cold was about to enter a team that was too fast for them. So, with a good look of justice proven as part of their track record, things would prove to be in their favor.

They all had been in their seats by this time with roughly 240 seconds left to landing time. It was a bit of wind three prior to landing; otherwise, landing was smooth. The pilot had put on the fasten seatbelt lights and had advanced his verbal of the city and the names of the airport; the pilot had even revealed the temperatures. The landing gear was in use now.

The tarmac of the runway was smooth.

The other plane for the staff landed almost right after the flight crew was eventfully admirable of his occupation also about the passengers that had been a second family to him.

So they after going to their hanger; they drank to pass time by while waiting for the other staff members to land.

This part of the day would be dedicated to the easy parts of their very own lives.

The four men from Chico's security staff had reached; jet-lagged four men with black caps and coats waited by the stairs with winter coats on their arm. Each of the men helped the men into their coats. The last plane would stay right outside the hangar.

Senator Chow, Mrs. Chow, Chico, and the rest of the staff all welcomed the men with open arms. Before being briefed, the hangar was combed to make the conversation that would be had would be basically history after the staff shut its doors.

The four men began briefing staff. First was the situation of the weapons. After that was the murder, where the guns were left was black lined kind of. The attack itself was now being shared. The men were asked was there any witnesses or counter attacks. To whereas the men answer was the same which was negative. They each were given refills. Julius had just taken three tokes on his newly rolled blunt by now. Everyone was socializing like old friends do.

There was going to be prosperity once this staff said there would be. Senator Chow gave a speech in Massachusetts, showing the difference between a killer and a murderer to which a murderer he described as a monster. Senator Chow went onto describe a killer more as a best that kills to supply for their young or for sole survival. The team after the speech left Massachusetts for North Dakota. On the flight, they ate and prepared. Senator Chow gave a memorable speech of the land and occupants turn being new to protect the supplier, Earth. Then to Arizona, they arrived where this was where the Senator said Americans are great because we care for all positive people. The audience ate all of it up.

Now reaching home sweet home, Nevada, the senator sat at home and had watched as the news showed election scores around the country; Senator Chow won popular votes over his opponents easily. As for electoral votes, the results were in, and the next president of the free world wife would/will name Divaress Chow.

ABOUT THE AUTHOR

C lifton Anselmo Fahie Jr., nicknamed "Deh Poopaz," was born on September 21, 1974, on St. Thomas, USVI, and is very fond of thoroughbred race horses and is a Rastafarian.